SPACE MATH

by Judith Bauer Stamper
Illustrated by Vince Andriani

SCHOLASTIC INC.
New York   Toronto   London   Auckland   Sydney   Mexico City   New Delhi   Hong Kong

A spaceship is about to blast off. It will take a long trip to far-off planets. There are five crew members on the ship. They all have jobs to do.

The ship needs one more crew member. Someone has to keep count of things. Can you be crew member number six?

You don't need to pack a bag. You don't have to bring food. All you need is your brain. Hurry up! Jump on the ship. We're off to do SPACE MATH!

Add the Aliens

Wow! Our spaceship flies fast! We're on our way to a place that no one has ever seen before. All around, the sky is dotted with stars. The ship speeds toward a big planet with five beautiful rings around it.

Look at the funny aliens on the rings. They have green and purple stripes. It's your job to count the aliens. How many aliens do you see?

Get a pencil and paper. Write the number. Write the number word, too.

[Check your answers on page 24.]

The ship flashes through space.
Falling stars streak by. One, two, three,
four, five, six!

What's that glow in front of the ship?
It's another planet. The ship slows down
to take a closer look.

There are more aliens to count on this planet. Each one has a body that glows. The aliens are red, yellow, green, white, and orange. They are so light that they float!

Count how many aliens there are on this planet. Then write the number. Write the number word, too.

Look, one of them sees you and waves! *[Check your answers on page 24.]*

The ship speeds up again. Oh, no! Flames are shooting out of the back. What went wrong? The ship will have to make a crash landing!

This planet looks big and safe. But something is going on. Lots of aliens are here. They are all shapes and sizes. Some are tall and thin. Some are short and round. Some have four arms.

This is your biggest job yet. Count the aliens on this planet. Then write the number. Write the number word, too.

Can you add up all the aliens you have seen so far? How many aliens did you count? *[Check your answers on page 24.]*

First Place in Space

The ship lands on the planet with a *BUMP!* and *BANG!* Two crew members jump out to find out what is wrong with the ship. They go to work to fix it. Inside the ship, everyone looks out to watch the aliens.

Look! A Space Scooter Race is about to begin. The eleven aliens are ready to race. How many are in purple scooters? How many are in yellow scooters? How many are in red scooters? Write the numbers and the number words.

BOOM! BOOM! BOOM! The race is on! *[Check your answers on page 24.]*

The space scooters race around the planet in a big circle in the sky. A yellow scooter flies out in front. It glides along smoothly. Next comes a purple scooter on a blaze of blue light.

Smoke billows out from the scooter in last place. It jerks and jumps, making *CLICK! CLANG! CLACK!* noises.

See the red scooter? Now it is in sixth place. But it is speeding up. How many scooters are behind it? How many scooters are in front of it? Write the answers. Write the number words, too.

Do you think the alien on the red scooter can win? *[Check your answers on page 24.]*

The red scooter wins! The alien jumps out of his ship and waves all four arms in the air!

The other scooters zoom across the finish line.

How many scooters will cross the finish line?

How many yellow scooters will finish the race?

How many purple scooters will cross the finish line?

Write the numbers to answer
the questions.

Write the number words, too.

[Check your answers on page 24.]

Countdown to Blastoff!

BANG! SLAM! BAM! The two crew members jump back inside the ship. They fixed the problem. Now, the ship is in tip-top shape and ready for takeoff.

The crew members begin the jobs they have to do before blastoff. One checks the gas. Another pushes the buttons. Three others flip the switches. We're ready to fly!

But who will do the countdown? Everyone looks at you. That's your job. See the flashing red button? It's time to start the countdown!

Ten!
Nine!
Eight!
Outside the window, we can see
the aliens. They are coming toward
our spaceship!

Seven!

Six!

Five!

Keep counting! Don't stop to look at the aliens in the window. Don't count the aliens! Don't stop the countdown!

Four!
Three!
Two!
Our spaceship begins to rumble.
Buttons blink, buzzers buzz, and beepers
beep. Smoke and fire shoot out. The
aliens run to their space scooters.

One!

Blast off!

With a shudder and a shake, our ship rises up off the ground. Blast off! The spaceship shoots into space! Outside the window, aliens on their space scooters wave good-bye.

How many aliens wave good-bye? Write the number and the number word.

[Check your answers on page 24.]

At last, our spaceship heads home.
What is that bright glow? It's the sun.
How many planets go around the sun?
   Write the number. Write the number
word, too. *[Check your answers on page 24.]*

Now find our planet — it's as easy as counting one, two, three! The third planet from the sun is Earth, our home world. Soon, the ship will land on it.

Good work, crew! There is just one more space math job for you to do.

Get ready to count down to touchdown! Start the count:

Ten, nine, eight, seven, six, five, four, three, two, one . . .

Touchdown!

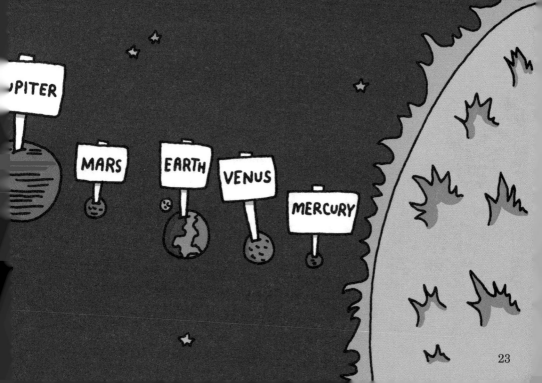

Phonics Reader 49 ★ Words to Sound Out

s-blends	l-blends
scooter	blast
sky	blink
smoke	clack
smoothly	clang
space	click
speeding	closer
stars	flames
start	flashes
switches	flicking
	flip
	fly
	glides
	glow
	place
	planets
	slows

Phonics Reader 49 ★ Words to Remember

eight   eleven   five   four   six

Phonics Reader 49 ★ Story Words

aliens	Earth	good-bye
color	front	paper

SPACE MATH Answers:

page 5:   4 four
page 7:   5 five
page 9:   11 eleven, 20 twenty
page 11:   4 four, 6 six, 1 one

page 13: 5 five, 5 five
page 14: 8 eight, 4 four, 3 three
page 21: 8 eight
page 22: 9 nine